CHINONYEREM O

Chinonyerem Odimba is a Nigeria-born, Bristol-based playwright, director and poet. Her work for theatre includes *Joanne* and *Amongst the Reeds* for Clean Break and The Yard, a modern retelling of *Twist* for Theatre Centre, and *Medea* at Bristol Old Vic. Her play *Princess & The Hustler* toured across the UK for Eclipse Theatre, Bristol Old Vic and Hull Truck, and her community play *The Seven Ages of Patience* premiered at Kiln Theatre, London.

Chinonyerem was the Writer-in-Residence at Live Theatre/Northumbria University for 2018–2019, and is currently Associate Artist at Live Theatre.

Her work has been shortlisted for several awards including the Adrienne Benham Award, Alfred Fagon Award, and the Bruntwood Playwriting Award. She is winner of the 2018 Sonia Friedman Award for a new play *How to Walk on the Moon* written for C4 and Talawa Theatre. Chinonyerem is currently is under commission for an adaptation of *The Prince and the Pauper* for Watermill Theatre, and a new musical play *Black Love* for Paines Plough.

Her work for radio and television includes the thirty-minute drama *Adulting* for 4Stories and Channel 4.

She has been as an Assistant Director and Director for Bristol Old Vic and Theatre503.

Other Titles in this Series

Mike Bartlett
ALBION
BULL
GAME
AN INTERVENTION
KING CHARLES III
VASSA *after* Gorky
WILD

Jez Butterworth
THE FERRYMAN
JERUSALEM
JEZ BUTTERWORTH PLAYS: ONE
MOJO
THE NIGHT HERON
PARLOUR SONG
THE RIVER
THE WINTERLING

Caryl Churchill
BLUE HEART
CHURCHILL PLAYS: THREE
CHURCHILL PLAYS: FOUR
CHURCHILL PLAYS: FIVE
CHURCHILL: SHORTS
CLOUD NINE
DING DONG THE WICKED
A DREAM PLAY *after* Strindberg
DRUNK ENOUGH TO SAY I LOVE YOU?
ESCAPED ALONE
FAR AWAY
GLASS. KILL. BLUEBEARD'S
    FRIENDS. IMP.
HERE WE GO
HOTEL
ICECREAM
LIGHT SHINING IN
    BUCKINGHAMSHIRE
LOVE AND INFORMATION
MAD FOREST
A NUMBER
PIGS AND DOGS
SEVEN JEWISH CHILDREN
THE SKRIKER
THIS IS A CHAIR
THYESTES *after* Seneca
TRAPS

Fiona Doyle
ABIGAIL
COOLATULLY
DELUGE
THE STRANGE DEATH OF JOHN DOE

Ifeyinwa Frederick
THE HOES

Natasha Gordon
NINE NIGHT

debbie tucker green
BORN BAD
DEBBIE TUCKER GREEN PLAYS: ONE
DIRTY BUTTERFLY
EAR FOR EYE
HANG
NUT
A PROFOUNDLY AFFECTIONATE,
    PASSIONATE DEVOTION TO
    SOMEONE (– *NOUN*)
RANDOM
STONING MARY
TRADE & GENERATIONS
TRUTH AND RECONCILIATION

Vicky Jones
THE ONE
TOUCH

Anna Jordan
CHICKEN SHOP
FREAK
POP MUSIC
THE UNRETURNING
WE ANCHOR IN HOPE
YEN

Arinzé Kene
GOD'S PROPERTY
GOOD DOG
LITTLE BABY JESUS
    & ESTATE WALLS
MISTY

Lucy Kirkwood
BEAUTY AND THE BEAST
    with Katie Mitchell
BLOODY WIMMIN
THE CHILDREN
CHIMERICA
HEDDA *after* Ibsen
IT FELT EMPTY WHEN THE
    HEART WENT AT FIRST BUT
    IT IS ALRIGHT NOW
LUCY KIRKWOOD PLAYS: ONE
MOSQUITOES
NSFW
TINDERBOX

Amy Ng
ACCEPTANCE
SHANGRI-LA

Chinonyerem Odimba
AMONGST THE REEDS
PRINCESS & THE HUSTLER

Janice Okoh
EGUSI SOUP
THREE BIRDS

Danusia Samal
OUT OF SORTS

Sam Steiner
KANYE THE FIRST
LEMONS LEMONS LEMONS
    LEMONS LEMONS
A TABLE TENNIS PLAY
YOU STUPID DARKNESS!

Jack Thorne
2ND MAY 1997
BUNNY
BURYING YOUR BROTHER IN
    THE PAVEMENT
A CHRISTMAS CAROL *after* Dickens
HOPE
JACK THORNE PLAYS: ONE
JUNKYARD
LET THE RIGHT ONE IN
    after John Ajvide Lindqvist
MYDIDAE
THE SOLID LIFE OF SUGAR WATER
STACY & FANNY AND FAGGOT
WHEN YOU CURE ME
WOYZECK *after* Büchner

Phoebe Waller-Bridge
FLEABAG

Chinonyerem Odimba

UNKNOWN RIVERS

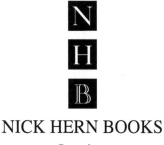

NICK HERN BOOKS

London

www.nickhernbooks.co.uk

A Nick Hern Book

Unknown Rivers first published in Great Britain in 2019 as a paperback original by Nick Hern Books Limited, The Glasshouse, 49a Goldhawk Road, London W12 8QP

Cover image: iStock.com/Andrea Izzotti

Designed and typeset by Nick Hern Books, London
Printed in Great Britain by Mimeo Ltd, Huntingdon, Cambridgeshire PE29 6XX

ISBN 978 1 84842 920 8

A CIP catalogue record for this book is available from the British Library

Woodland
CARBON
www.woodlandcarbon.co.uk
NICK HERN BOOKS
Printed on Carbon Captured paper

Unknown Rivers was first performed at Hampstead Theatre Downstairs, London, on 31 October 2019. The cast was as follows:

LEA	Renee Bailey
DEE	Doreene Blackstock
NENE	Nneka Okoye
LUNE	Aasiya Shah
Director	Daniel Bailey
Designer	Amelia Jane Hankin
Lighting	Martha Godfrey
Sound	Duramaney Kamara

To all the Black and Brown girls and women
whose softness is their strength.

Characters

NENE, *eighteen years old. Black British girl. Lives in a council flat with her mother Dee.*

DEE, *forty-five years old. Black British working-class woman. Moved to the UK at the age of seven from Nigeria.*

LEA, *nineteen years old. Black British woman. Works in an office job.*

LUNE, *nineteen years. Asian British woman. Works in the same office as Lea.*

Spaces

Dee's house is a small narrow house. Split into two floors, the first floor is made up of a hallway and front room as well as a kitchen – all the rooms have all the signs of excessive hoarding. The kitchen is to the left, and a front room to the right. The front room has two faux-leather sofas, which we can barely make out, as well as framed pictures of Nene in school uniform that balance on top of piles of magazines, portraits of a child, and a painted portrait of Dee that peeks out from behind one of the sofas. On one side of the room is an almost panoramic view of the skyline from a window that runs from one edge of wall to another. The windowsill is filled with an array of ceramic and glass ornaments, piles of *National Geographic* magazines, and other odd bits. On a small coffee table by the side of one of the sofas is a phone.

There is a smaller room at the back of the house – a playroom of sorts filled with shelving – full of toys – as well as remnants of sewing paraphernalia, a clothes dummy, reams/tubes of African material.

Down the hallway is a wallpaper of various maps. Maps of different parts of the local area, different parts of the local town, and maps of unknown rivers. Some maps are larger than others. At the end of the hallway is one large framed photograph of Dee and Nene – sixteen years before the moment we meet them.

Upstairs, there is a bathroom and two bedrooms. One is Dee's – a plainly decorated room bursting to full with broken bits of furniture and a rickety wardrobe in one corner.

The other bedroom is Nene's bedroom – small, girly, neat.

The World Outside.

Notes

An ellipsis (…) indicates a trailing-off or pause at the end of dialogue.

A forward slash (/) indicates an overlap in speech or a self-interruption – one thought interrupted by another.

This text went to press before the end of rehearsals and so may differ slightly from the play as performed.

ACT ONE

1.

Two young women enter. NENE *and* LEA *stand close together. They both stare ahead for a long beat.*

There is something uncomfortable in the silence.

NENE *starts rummaging in her bag.*

LEA *takes one step forward.*

NENE. Wait please / please wait.

LEA. Yes.

NENE. I…

LEA. Are you counting and breathing?

NENE. Yes. I think so.

    LEA *moves towards* NENE.

LEA. This is it / Nene.

NENE. I'm not sure / about…

LEA. What?

NENE. It's just / hard…

LEA. What?

NENE. To get back past five /

LEA. Okay but five is good Nene. If you're feeling a five then /

NENE. I'm / trying…

LEA. You're doing it / really!

    Beat.

    You need another minute?

LEA *moves back to her position next to* NENE.

NENE. Yeah that's all. A minute / to just…

    Beat.

LEA. We are here now / Nene.

    Outside!

NENE. I know…

    But the feeling…

    Creeps up on me…

    Drips into my mind y'know.

    And I'm like…

LEA. I know!

NENE. Look I want to yeah. Move faster. Yeah. Want to not let you down. Yeah. Like you made this happen / for me.

    The thing is that I'm getting that feeling…

    And I want to say no but…

    No.

    But I'm getting that feeling. That everything is too open. Too much space…

    And I think I've forgotten something.

LEA. What's *real*?

NENE. Even put my outfit out last night so I wouldn't have to stress this morning.

LEA. You look nice Nene.

    Beat.

    Are you still counting? What number are you feeling now Nene? Are you feeling more than five? Six maybe?…

NENE. –

LEA. What do you think you've forgotten?

NENE. I don't know. I won't know until I check again will I?

  The thing is I don't think I can really go any further unless
  I check. You get that don't you? You get what I'm saying Lea.

  But out here... I mean people are moving so fast...

  And I need to have a good look y'know just in case. I can't
  just go out for the day without being sure I have everything.
  Y'know. You get it don't you / Lea?

LEA. Course babes!

  We can move over there.

  There.

  I can hold your bag whilst you check. It's cool. Cos then
  you'll know and that feeling will go and we can count and
  five is good.

NENE. On the edge / of it.

LEA. I got that extra bit of commission at work dinned I?
  Been saving it. Going to treat you Nene. I want to buy you
  something *exotic* like *spaghetti alle vongole*.

NENE. What? That sounds wrong!

LEA. It's...

  It does doesn't it...

  But look the twinnies are back.

  LEA *breaks into a dance. A familiar routine.* NENE *joins in
  for a beat.*

  They laugh.

NENE. Six.

LEA. Really?

NENE. Yeah I think so.

LEA. Yes!

LEA *takes a step forward/away from* NENE.

Let's go over there…

Beat.

LEA *stands in front of* NENE *as she rummages through her bag.*

NENE. Sorry / Lea.

LEA. It's cool / Nene.

Fine.

Honestly…

Long beat.

NENE. Okay.

Everything is here. Nothing missing. Everything is there.
Purse.
Cards.
Tissues.
And more tissues.
Chewing gum.
Nail file.
Concealer.
Phone.
Charger.
Coconut oil.
Headphones.
Anti-bac for…

LEA. We're going to have so much fun / today Nene.

NENE. Just for a few hours you said.

LEA. Yes. Proper grown-up lunch at the place I showed you on
the map.

I've been saving…

I mean who has to save for a meal out when they work full time? I might as well be working a shoe shop for the amount I get paid!

It's not far Nene. Ten minutes / that way.

NENE. Two hundred metres turn left. Four hundred metres turn left. Half a mile down that one road, and it should be on the right. Il Forte Italiano. Good rating on TripAdvisor.

– Slow service but no reports of food poisoning in 2019.

LEA. That's it.

Then maybe…

Beat.

We can stop when you need to Nene.

LEA *is a little distracted looking at her phone during the following speech.*

NENE. Lea. This is the furthest I've been in forever.

It'll be alright won't it?

I mean it's just going to be a nice day isn't it?

Beat.

But if you don't mind I could just hold on to your top…
By the elbow…

LEA. I'm here.

NENE. I'm going to hold on to you tight yeah when we walk in. Just in case…

LEA. Course!

NENE. It's only in case…
In case it all flows too fast and everything washes away.

LEA *looks up and hard at* NENE.

LEA. *– No reported food poisoning for a whole 2019.*

They can take all my monies!

NENE. We can't be the first though so no seafood yeah just in case.

LEA. But spaghetti alle vongole is good you know…

NENE. It still sounds weird!

NENE takes a step forward. They link arms.

They exeunt.

2.

The front garden. DEE stands amongst an array of soft toys, and half-played games, and thrown-around dolls. She slowly lifts herself up.

DEE. If anyone ever tells you that having children is easy, don't listen.

Really. Block your ears. Hold them shut. Don't even pretend to listen. Don't even pretend to hear them. Work your way out of the vicinity of that conversation, and be glad that you nevar heard anything past the words –

– No, it's easy! They give you joy.

It is a lie. It is a lie that most people tell long after their own children have grown, and long left their house. Watch those ones! They're the ones that say shit like that. They will tell you anything now, they don't have to wipe pen off of their clean walls. They don't have to wake up to dry snot in their eye, which may I remind you is quickly followed by the worst case of conjunctivitis ever seen by your local medical practice. They are long past having to pick up poo-poo-streaked pants or worse still, the actual poo-poo when they miss the toilet altogether.

Yeah those ones…

Watch them talk about how children bring a certain kind of peace to your life.

Chineke! What peace?

You see peace here? Let me tell you the peace they are talking about is the two hours of straight sleep you get once a week. That's it. That's peace? I remember when peace was walking to my secretary's job in *Paree* in the early morning, and stopping in one of those fancy bakeries for coffee and *croissant*. That was the best kind of peace.

This wahala!

This is something else.

But tell me to live without har. Tell me to imagine a day without har. Tell me to see beyond that big thing in my chest that started growing the day she was born. I dare you to tell me to know anything else but har. Har ways. Har screw-up face when she doesn't like something. Something cold. Or something hot like pepper. Tell me to not sit here and look at har every strand of hair growing from har skin. And not wish every day that I could find a way to bottle up the smell of har after she has spent a whole hour running and jumping puddles. Tell me to live not dreaming all my dreams for har /

Babygirl cries.

And this noise…

Because that is what it is. Don't let them tell you you can hear anything in this other than noise.

Simple noise.

And it will get worse in a minute. When she realises that I haven't run in. Jumped to har attention. Felt har trouble all the way through the walls.

She leans in towards the house. Listening.

She will cry louder and stronger, and all this noise will do…

It will make my heart softer until…

I will run in now…

I will give in to my soft heart and still feel somehow that
I have won. Because I have you see. I, Dee Okoye, I have
won in this life. A new thing…

And even when I tell myself I can't do it again. I know I can.
I know I can do it better. Get it right this time.

Beat.

Cry gets louder.

Told you it would get louder.

3.

NENE *and* LEA *stand either side of a table.* NENE*'s eyes are
fixed ahead – looking at something/nothing.*

NENE. This place…

LEA. Told you. Posh yeah.

NENE. And there's so many people. And they're looking…

LEA. A window table. That's what I told them. But I explained /
to them you know /

NENE. I'm trying not to look back. Cos then I'll think I've
forgotten something. That's what I'm thinking… that must
be it. I haven't forgotten anything important. We checked.
I'm trying to tell myself it isn't real. And I've checked…

NENE *holds back tears. Pulls a tissue from her bag.*

LEA. Nene…

NENE. Wait…

LEA. Nene…

NENE. Wait / I know.

LEA. I shouldn't have / rushed you.

NENE. The thing is I was going to ask if I could wait by the
door a bit longer…
But your face Lea…
And I was getting that kind of seven feeling but then you
said –

*People don't look. They're busy eating. Looking at their
date, wife, the waiter…*

But I can see everyone is looking…

So I was like…

No.

Too many people in here. But out here. Too many people /

LEA. From here we can see everything happening outside. We
can see the cars drive past. And there won't be too many cars
because this is a quiet road. I checked. And we'll see people
just doing you know…

Like when we're at yours. By the window. Watching. And
we'll guess where they live like we always do and…

Pause.

LUNE *is walking quickly towards them. Waving.*

LUNE. Lea!

LUNE *is now standing in front of them.*

LEA. Lune…

Fuck!

What are you / doing here?

LUNE. You didn't think I was going to miss out on a boujee
lunch did you?

NENE. Lea?

NENE *is gasping for air.*

LEA. No. Lune… you can't / be here.

LUNE. I've been dying to come to this place. Great reviews!

LEA. Lune / please...

LUNE. Lea. I...

I can't be at home today. My auntie from *home* is coming to visit...

I'd rather be here with you.

LEA. Lune you can't...

Nene...

NENE. There's too many people...

LEA. You're going to have to go Lune.

LUNE. What?

NENE. Why would you do this Lea?

LEA. I didn't...

Please. Lune. Please just go.

NENE. You said...

LUNE. Seriously Lea?

NENE *gasps for air.*

I can't be there Lea /

NENE. I can't be here...

NENE*'s head darts back and forth – panicked – looking for the way out.*

It's all flowing too fast /

LEA. Wait...

Nene...

NENE *gasping for more air.*

Beat.

NENE. You said...

LEA. I didn't know…

NENE. I don't want to…

It's going too fast…

NENE *holds a tissue to her nose.*

LUNE. Shit!

LEA. See!

LEA *moves to touch/hold* NENE.

NENE *flinches.*

LUNE. I thought maybe you wouldn't…

We could / all hang.

LUNE *moves towards* LEA.

LEA *flinches.*

LEA. I didn't ask Lune to come Nene.

LUNE. No you didn't!

LEA. You have to believe me…

Beat.

NENE. I can't y'know Lea.

Y'know that I can't…

NENE *throws her head back again – pinches her nose.*

LUNE. She needs to stop the bleeding /

LEA. She knows!

NENE. I can't!

NENE *wants to move. She just can't get her legs to move.*
Beat.

She gives up struggling to get her body to do something.
Long beat.

LUNE *holds her hand out.*

LUNE. I'm /

LEA. Nene. This is Lune. She's a friend from work.

NENE. –

LEA. Lune this is Nene. My twinny from time. My right- and left-hand girl. My best friend since nursery...

NENE. –

LUNE. Nene...

I was just going to have lunch with you.

I thought...

Sorry...

LEA. Nene...

LUNE. It's nice in here.

LEA. You can have the chair that looks out of the window.

Beat.

We can go out anytime.

Are you still counting? /

NENE. Maybe we could go back.

It's not the restaurant...

LUNE. We could sit!

Beat.

Nene...

We could sit and I know this thing that you can do...

With a cold spoon...

My mum does it sometimes when we get nosebleeds. It runs in my family too.

LEA. It's not like that Lune /

NENE. A spoon?

LUNE. Yes an ice-cold spoon.

Sit.

I promise it'll work.

I'll call someone over to get us ice water. For the spoon /

NENE. No! I don't really want to be looked at like / this.

LUNE. Okay…

LEA. Lune!

LUNE. Nene I didn't mean to…

LEA. I wanted today to be good. Special.

Fuck!

NENE. It's stopped.

NENE tucks the bloodied tissues in her bag. Gets a fresh tissue out and checks her nose for any more blood.

Long beat.

LUNE picks up a menu lying on the table. Holds it out to NENE, who tentatively takes it.

LEA. We can go…

NENE. But people are looking…

LUNE. So what if they are! Girl if you've got it…

LEA. She's not talking about / that!

LUNE pulls a face at LEA to suggest she keep quiet.

NENE. What? If I've got what?

LUNE. Your outfit of the day course!

NENE. Me?

LUNE. Yes you! We're hungry and you're serving.

LEA. Lune not now /

LUNE. You look fucking golden / girl.

NENE. Golden?

LEA. No. Lune you love to chat shit you know that?

NENE. It's Jill / Scott.

LUNE. Thank you Nene. Someone with actual taste.

Classic tune!

LEA. I'm just saying why don't you try not talking in gimmickry all the time!

LUNE. For fuck's sakes I'm having fun Lea. Remember that thing they used to do in the eighties. Fun. It's making a comeback /

LEA. You're being a bit...

LUNE. What? This is you all over. Making shit up as you go along. All these rules about what's alright, and what's not alright. Girl bye!

LEA. Stop your drama Lune.

LUNE *sulks*.

NENE. People are looking / at us.

Lea...

LEA. We can go out for a minute...

If you're...

NENE. Four. I think...

LUNE. For what?

Long beat.

Anyway I need to use the toilet and I might not be back for a while...

LUNE *pulls out a packet of antibacterial wet wipes from her bag*.

It feels like putting my life at risk every time I go to a public toilet.

NENE. Germs?

LUNE. Yes. All those stains…

LEA. Ugh!

LUNE. Grow up Lea.

LEA. Why are you being so salty with me when you're the one that's just turned up here?

LUNE. Wow!

LEA. I was joking…

LUNE. You're always going on about people not taking you seriously but sometimes…

LEA. I only say that stuff about people at work anyways. You know / how they are.

LUNE. Yes yes / I know.

LEA. I thought you got how unhappy I am there.

I have to go to that fucking office every day and pretend that all their fucking microaggressions aren't slowly killing me. And the only person I can really talk to about it is you, and now you're being like this about it?

I won't chat to you about it again!

LUNE. I didn't mean I don't want you to talk to me… I… maybe do something about it.

LUNE *makes a gesture to make the peace with* LEA.
LEA *refuses*.

You're such a child Lea!

NENE. No. She's not. She's not that.

LUNE. Well as much as I'm enjoying being the raspberry in this situ right now.

LEA. You mean gooseberry / Lune.

LUNE. No. I definitely mean raspberry because I'm way too fine and sweet to be a gooseberry. And that waitress has been hovering to take our order for about a decade. Order me a spaghetti alle vongole with an extra side of naughty waitress!

LUNE *flounces off – exiting.*

NENE *and* LEA *watch* LUNE *in amazement as she walks away.*

LEA. Nene I would never do that…

I wish I hadn't told Lune we were coming here today.

NENE. Is Lune always so…?

Talks a lot too…

LEA. Not doing your head in?

NENE. I don't know…
Maybe…

Maybe Lune is right and you do need to do something about work /

LEA. You know I can't. My parents worked so hard to save up for my uni and then I let them down by dropping out after a year. Do you know how proud they are that I have this job in this swanky big publishing house now? Imagine if I failed at this too? /

NENE. But they wouldn't want you to be feeling this bad. If you told them /

LEA. Nene you know I can't! You know that's how it works. That's how it is for girls like us. Things we can't say…

NENE. What are we going to tell Lune about me?

I don't want to spoil it for you Lea…

LEA. We'll have *fun*. Promise.

Ignore Lune.

NENE. –

LEA. This isn't pressure. I don't want to do that to you… This is just me chatting. Like wanting things to be okay *for you.*

You might not get this Nene but I *miss* you yeah. I miss the
days we used to hang out by the Greek bakery hoping they
would give us free pasties just before they closed. Remember
your favourites were those spinach and feta ones. *So crispy
on the outside, so delicate on the inside* that's what you used
to say like you were some TV chef. And you used to say you
were going to open your own bakery one day. With the
biggest fanciest cakes this side of the North Circ. You used
to say that all the time. I miss *that*.

And no pressure yeah because today…
For today…
But I wish that for you…
And I can wait for however long it takes to get that *you* back.
And I'll still come round every Wednesday and Friday and
we'll still have dinner on our laps and watch TV like we're
some old couple and that won't change yeah. That won't
change and all I'm really chatting about now is the things
that…
Stuff that I dream of for you.
'Cept *today* you will be able to remember all the overpriced
pasta we're going to eat and know it was real, and it will feel
that bit more real every minute, and you'll know that you can
do this…

NENE. Today is nothing Lea. You must know that. Today is just
like all those other days you talked and talked at me. Except
this time…

Today is about me making *you* happy Lea. And tomorrow I'll
go back to being me. Only smelling the air outside when
I catch it once in a while. Watching the days pass, each shade
of sky every day from the window.

LEA. And we can do today again. Another day.

NENE. Maybe…

LUNE *enters*.

LUNE. Let's eat bishes!

4.

The front room. DEE *lies on her belly. Pieces of paper –
good-quality sheets of art paper – around her.*

DEE. The thing…

The thing I nevar got was the drawing. I mean it's a skill
you're juss meant to have as a mother. Draw a tree. Draw
a face. Draw an elephant. Draw a spaceship. I couldn't draw
even a fish.

And worst of it is that I used to see har little disappointed
face. Like that look itself had been drawn on har own face.
Like cartoon disappointment. And she would say –

*– What is that Mummy?
What is that meant to be?*

And I wouldn't know what to say. I would open my mouth to
say anything to take that disappointment from har but what
do you say to a child? I was not interested at all in most of
my art classes at school. What for? My parents would have
not had anything to do with it. My parents nevar did things
like that with me. I come from a place where *artist* was once
a dirty word. Another word for *degenerate*. Another word for
an unfulfilled life…

I couldn't say any of that so instead I would hold it up like
this –

DEE *holds up a piece of paper with a child's drawing.*

And say –

See what you want to see!

Then she would give me the other look. Like Mum you're
bullshitting me and I am not playing.

Never understood how young children and old people have
the same way of looking at you that can reduce you to salt.

But we would draw nevertheless. Me and her rolling on the
floor like this…

Drawing.

DEE *starts to roll around in the confined space of her front room. Stopping and starting at her own will during the following speech.*

And we would roll and for those few minutes. For that moment. In that minute. Of that day. As we rolled we would connect in a different way. Pens in hand. Laughing and rolling. Like two parts of the earth coming together. Two rivers meeting for the first time.
We would roll.
Roll and roll.
Me and her...
Rolling...

Rolling...

Rivers meeting...

Rolling rivers...

Greeting...

Unknown rivers that we were...

In our own world of chalk and crayon.

Rolling...

DEE *stops rolling as a pile of stuff topples over. Water seeps through the floor.*

And the worst thing to say as a mother is the things you miss. I know. But I miss that, I miss that girl. I miss who she was. And who I was. And all that she was. And I was. And I want us to carry on rolling like this...

Beat.

But those happy skin-warm rivers stopped and what she was got washed away and me...

Cold harsh currents. Cold hard water still has me rolling. Every single day after has me rolling. But that's my due. That's my punishment...

DEE *carefully replaces the things that have fallen. Trying to stem the flow of water.*

And when she swelled… when it swells… this water…
it took us both with it.

But it gave us something too. It gave us her.

This Babygirl inside making all this noise…

5.

NENE *and* LUNE *sit at the café/restaurant table.*

NENE *strokes the carefully ironed white tablecloth meditatively.*

NENE. It's so quiet now…

LUNE. Because they're closed!

    LUNE *yawns.*

NENE. Everything…

    Spaced out…

    NENE *yawns.*

LUNE. We need to go Nene.

    I don't think Lea will be able to get them to give us more time…

    I know you need more time but…

NENE. I need to stay here.

    Beat.

LUNE. Lea is so good to you. It's so sweet.

NENE. Yeah. We went to school / together.

LUNE. I think you're really lucky. I don't really have friends
    like that. Not old friends like that. New friends but not…
    Friends that would do anything for you. Like this.
    Nene…

This was one of the first things I knew about her. *You…*
How she spends every Wednesday and Friday with *you*.
Doesn't ever tell me what you're doing but has never not
been at *yours* after work on those days. And trust me I have
tried to get her out a number of times on a Wednesday
because there's this bangin' night that goes on just past the
railway bridge but it's not the sort of place you should go to
on your own…
But no!
Every time she chooses *you*.

NENE. I wouldn't stop her. From going anywhere. She knows
that. I would be okay with it…

LUNE. To be honest, I used to think she was in love with you /
or something.

NENE. It's not like that!

LUNE. I know. That's what I'm saying.

I was just trying to work it out /

NENE. You can ask her to do things with you too.

I don't make her come over. I don't need anyone feeling
sorry for me / y'know.

LUNE. She said you don't go out much / ever.

Beat.

NENE. Did she?

LUNE. Like you're a bit of a homebody…

Keep yourself to yourself.

You know…

I don't know anything about you other than you have a kid
and don't really go out.

NENE. And?

LUNE. I don't get it…
You're young and you're fit. To be honest I was expecting
you to be a bit…

NENE. You don't know me.

LUNE. Yes that's what I'm saying…

Anyway you look prettier than I thought you would for a shy teenage mum…

NENE. I'm not that… shy.

LUNE. Issa compliment.

LEA *enters*.

LEA. Large Sprite.

NENE. Thanks.

LUNE. Where's mine?

LEA. They thought it might help Nene.

LUNE. You could have asked for me too.

LEA. This isn't about you Lune.

Go ask the waiter yourself. He's just over by the bar.

LUNE *flounces off*.

Beat.

NENE. Do you feel sorry for me?

LEA. What?

NENE. I don't need you to feel sorry for me.

LEA. You're my best mate!

NENE. Lune said…

LEA. Nene. Truss me the last thing you want to do is actually listen to Lune /

NENE. She's talking like she knows my life /

LEA. All I told Lune was that you had a young daughter. Just so I wouldn't keep having to say why I don't / you don't come out.

NENE. But your life is yours. Every day of the week yeah...
You can go out on Wednesdays or Fridays if you want to.
We can switch up the days. You've got to live Lea. One of us
has to live.

LEA. We're both *alive* actually. And today / even more.

NENE. Today you're happy because I'm out. But tomorrow...

NENE *is trying to look hard at something.*

LEA. Then cool. Make me happy for today. I want it to be
something we can talk about for a few weeks until the next
time / you give in.

NENE *suddenly ducks down on the ground. Trying to crawl
under the table.*

Nene!

NENE. He's watching...

Looking again...

There...

Can you see his eyes looking for me?

LEA. Who?

NENE. He's out there...

LEA. Who can you see Nene?

NENE. I didn't want to tell you...

I think he's been there the whole time.

Watching from outside...

I can see the jacket...

The red lining...

I remember how he always used to hang it up so that you
could see the red lining...

NENE *reaches in a pocket for a tissue. She holds it to
her nose.*

LEA. Do you want me to go outside and look to see if there's anyone there?

LUNE *enters holding a drink.*

LUNE. What da fuck?

Is she...?

LEA *holds a finger to her mouth to keep* LUNE *from talking on.*

NENE. You can see it from here. A cream jacket. Collar turned up. Red lining. He is inside that jacket...

LEA. I'll go and look...

LEA *exits.*

NENE *pushes herself further under the table.*

Long beat.

LUNE. So has Lea told you how we met? Honestly the best story. I was working at the agency, trying to be an assistant to some prick with the skinniest legs I ever saw on a man or child, and they get this new assistant in. And she's the assistant. And from the moment we clocked each other...

I couldn't believe that there was another brown face staring at me to be fair I mean this is an agency that works all around the world but their staff basically all come from the one square mile in East London. And I was so shocked that I actually walked up to her. And poked her. Not like an old-school Facebook poke, like a proper poke to just check she was real...

And from then, we were lunch buddies, then morning Tube buddies, and then gym buddies except that didn't last long, and now we're weekend buddies... I thought...

LUNE *sits down on the floor close to the table. Throughout* LUNE's *story,* NENE *seems to calm a little. Straightens up a little. Crawls out from under the table.*

And the thing is, like I was saying before, I don't have friends like that. Friends that do anything for you. I don't have that since I told everyone who I really was. My *friends* from before call it me *changing*. But I'm still me. But they don't know what to call me, and then they get all tongue-tied over words and acronyms and get embarrassed or scared and eventually they stop trying to work it out and leave…

NENE *spots something on* LUNE*'s thigh.*

NENE. Lune what are those marks?

LUNE *covers her legs quickly.*

LEA *enters and kneels on the floor too.*

LEA. Nene…

There's no one there. They've locked the door just in case…

LUNE. And some stick around hoping that one day I'll come to my senses and do the *normal* thing like them.

NENE. You can only be who you are…

LUNE *reaches into her bag, and pulls out a small bottle of rum.*

LUNE. I'll drink to that!

LEA. Just drink your Coke Lune!

LUNE. Oh you think I'm jokin'?

She pours a large splash into her glass. She holds it out to NENE.

I won't let anything happen to you. Swear on my life.

I'll get more glasses. Don't start without me!

LUNE *exits.*

LEA. You don't have to if you don't…

NENE *takes a big gulp of the drink.*

Okay!

They're trying to get ready to open tonight again. Nene we're going to have to leave soon. And I can't carry you out.

NENE. –

LEA. We can't stay here Nene…

NENE. Do you think Mum will be worried?

LEA. I didn't mean…

NENE. What if he goes there? To watch her? What if they go out and he follows them?

LEA. Your mum said they would stay in. Until you got home. You don't have to worry. They're safe. Honestly.

This is for her too remember.

LUNE *enters*.

LUNE (*talking into the air behind her*). Yeah yeah! It's an emergency. She's having a moment.

Chill!

LUNE *drops down to her knees holding two glasses of Coke. Hands one to LEA. Pours each a top-up of rum.*

Never had a lock-in in a restaurant before.

Cheers bishes!

LEA. Stop!

NENE. You're funny…

LUNE. See someone with an actual sense of humour!

Let's drink…

Wait!

LUNE *takes a sip of her drink.*

There is no fun in this glass.

She pours them all more rum until the bottle is empty!

LEA. Lune!

LUNE. Now we are literally drinking fun!

They all take a big mouthful of the concoction.

NENE. I like it!

LEA. Nene be careful…

NENE. Just cos I don't really like wine doesn't mean I don't like *this*!

LUNE. Yassss Nene!

LUNE *sticks her tongue out at* LEA. LEA *does the same back. They all laugh.*

NENE. You look happy Lea.

LEA. I'm bursting!

When was the last time we did anything like this? The twinnies out and about.

LUNE. Ahem!

LEA. And you too Lune.

LUNE. Well thank you Black Jesus, she's finally acknowledged me!

They all drink more.

NENE *lies on her back. She starts to roll along the ground.*

NENE. This reminds me of this thing me and Mum used to do.

She called it rolling rivers…

Said it was practice for when I became a mermaid.

LUNE. A what exactly?

LEA. What you don't know? This is Nene Okoye and she's a fucking mermaid!

LEA *and* LUNE *start rolling too. All laughing as they do.*

6.

Babygirl can be heard splashing.

DEE. Just a trickle really she said. The first time. Just a trickle down her nose.

Har standing there.

Sometimes these things happen I thought…

Maybe it's the dust at school.

But everything is clean here. It gets cleaned.

Okay I said…

But it wasn't just a trickle. It didn't stop for a while. Pouring in fact.

We could go to the doctor's…

No she said. I can't go anywhere.

Beat.

Until she could no longer hide it and she swelled…

And she came in here and told me. Told me that she was going to be a mother. I cried for har. I cried for my baby because which mother wouldn't. She was a child and now she was swelling. The heart already beating. Everything already formed. And she…

And she just stood there. I was waiting for all the excuses. For all the tears. For all the sorries. For all the weight of it to come crashing down on har. But she just stood there. With that look ageen. That look of disappointment ageen.

And she said juss those two words –

– You angry?

Beat.

So that was it. The start of people staring at us. Talking about things they don't know. People at work whispering…

And even though she has already stopped going to school; if adults are big-mouthed, children are much crueller.

We still have people poking their mouths where they are not wanted. Some days it's the school. But mostly now it is the social workers. They have the biggest mouths. Chat, chat, chatting about your business as if it is some kind of classical poetry they learned at school...

– *I came because the school / called.*

What about the school?

– *It is their duty / you know that. They have to raise any concerns / again...*

This particular new social worker is saying this only last week. Her mouth opening and closing like a *Placidochromis Phenochilus Mdoka White Lip*.

Creating a fuss over nothing / again.

The school knows everything they need to know. I say. They ring you because they can't get me to do what they want / right now.

Why do you have to do this to us every couple of months?

Why?

– *They would like to meet Nene. It's important.*

Always important.

She gets to nursery every day on time. Nene bathes her and oils her skin every morning. Combs her hair and brushes her teeth. And every Sunday she irons all her clothes for her. Ready for school. Always ready.

This is all good Nene / really. I say.

And she stands and waves at her. Every school day.

Big hands as fast as fans. Her head hot. Until we turn the corner. She is still waving. Every day.

She is so happy this little Babygirl.

What is there to be concerned about?

– *She is her mother and it's important…*

In my culture. Back in my town, it is not strange for children to be brought up by their grandparents, aunts…

Pause.

For them to take their grandchildren to school. To the market. Anywhere. It's normal. Grandparents do stuff like that. What is so different about here from *there*… Grandparents and grandchildren are the same everywhere we go.

– *But we are here and the school feels that they have a responsibility to inform us if we are not making progress.*

Eh eh!

– *The maps on the walls in the hallway…*

You've seen those maps / before. Have you not?

DEE *kisses her teeth.*

– *Yes. There seems to be more…*
Maps…

She goes to gymnastics now. On a Saturday morning. And sometimes a new soft-play place.
That's all. We need the *new* maps for that. New things. New maps to trace it. That's it. Then that way she knows the exact route. She can see the exact streets we are going up… from memory… the exact ones we're walking down.

I have told you this before…
The red pen is for the route we would take if there was an emergency. If something happened like an accident.
A crash.
Something that was stopping me and the little one from going the blue way. The usual way.
Something big though. Bigger than all of us.

That's why it's in red. Just in case…

And maybe one day…

– *One day… One day. That's all the school are saying…*

That is not all the school are saying!

Beat.

– That would be progress wouldn't it?

Beat.

– I just wanted to check…

We're fine / I'm fine.

– Sure?

Beat.

A trickle of blood runs down from DEE*'s nose.*

7.

NENE *is walking in circles. Looking anywhere and everywhere.*
LEA *and* LUNE *struggle to keep up.*

NENE *stops.*

LUNE *puts in headphones and starts to dance – lost in her own world.*

NENE. Where is this…?

LEA. Where?

NENE. I'm sure this is it… The place we used to buy all of them fake-gold earrings. The ones that looked proper.

You know where I mean…

Next to the shop we used to buy all those fake trainers from.

LEA. Different street / Nene.

NENE. No I remember!

It was here…

This road takes you towards Bounds Green and this street…

LEA. No it's not. This is where the old post office was…

Before it became another café where you can drink your frappumochoccino whilst you relax on the cushions that no one has ever washed and hundreds of people sit on every day.

NENE. It's not…

LEA. Look. That's the road that we used to walk down to get to the pool /

NENE. The pool?…

LEA. It doesn't matter…

Places change round here every five minutes at the moment…

NENE. I thought I could remember…

Y'know just remember. Without having to look at the maps.

LEA. I still get lost Nene /

NENE. At least you try…

LEA. You're trying today…

NENE. I'm lost…

This was my / our area. Where *we* did things. And now it's not even in my head any more. All I have is maps…

LEA. Nene don't think about it. You're doing so much already /

NENE. Lea I'm doing nothing.
I'm missing everything. And I can't do anything about it. Every time Babygirl does something new, I'm not there… First time on the swings. First time seeing a puppet show. First time seeing snow even.

What else am I going to miss?

LEA. You're doing so well. Nene. You plaited her hair for the first time. Taught her to sing nursery rhymes way before she got to school. Making cupcakes with her /

NENE. And who's going to teach her to swim?

It's our story. It's what makes us who we are. It's the way things have to be done from time. I come from somewhere, and now it looks like this is where…

Where *our story* is going to end.

What then Lea?

There seems to be music coming from LUNE*'s direction.*

NENE *and* LEA *turn to face* LUNE.

LUNE. Are you not going to dance with me?

LEA. Not now Lune.

NENE. I need to…

LUNE. Listen to this.

LUNE *holds out the headphones to* NENE.

Go on!

It's something my mum listens to. Makes me feel close to her…

Beat.

NENE *takes the headphones tentatively, and puts them on her ears.*

LEA. What is it? The music…

LUNE. Little Simz.

LEA. Your mum doesn't listen to that / Lune!

LUNE. Lea. This is a lot. She is / a lot.

LEA. Don't say that.

LUNE. What do you want to do today Lea?

LEA. What?

LUNE. *You.* What do *you* want?

LEA. I want her to fucking remember. I want her to fucking remember this place like all the other places we did things. The walls we sat on. The sound of the street. The sound of different streets.

Beat.

She's the only thing that makes me feel like I'm doing something right.

At work...

Home...

Us as twinnies was the best you know. Just us sitting on a wall or listening to tunes in my room. The way we could spend whole days together and still not feel like we've told each other everything. I want to feel that again. I want to feel like I'm getting something right.

When you're at school, everyone has the story that makes them stand out you know. Like someone's uncle who is in prison or someone's brother who is nearly a famous footballer.

Nene's story was about her mum teaching her how to swim /

LUNE. What about *you* Lea?

Beat.

LEA. I... I didn't have a story...

LUNE. Because of her?

LEA. No. This is about me. *My* mum. She loves me. But she says –

– It's about working hard. Working harder than everyone else. That's the only way to even have a chance in this country / this world.

So that's what I did. Worked hard. At school. At college and apart from Nene I had no friends. Then I got to uni and I was tired of trying so hard. I would think about my life and...

All that learning and I was still the last person to be given props for my grades. I tried you know. I tried to keep working but then I had...

I started having panic attacks. Like spending days in bed crying. Pretended to Nene I had bad flu for a few weeks...

And I left. I said I would start again after a while but I never went back. I couldn't.

But Mum was so disappointed. I could tell. She said even a few months of doing nothing would affect my job prospects.

So I tried even harder. To get out of bed. To smile...

I wanted to make my mum proud again. Started to apply for jobs.

NENE – *unseen by* LEA – *takes off the headphones.*

Girls like us don't get to take time...

We don't get to have a rest...

NENE. My mum taught me how to swim in that pool...
The same way that grandmother taught her.

She bought us both a new swimming costume. It had to be blue you see so that we would become almost invisible in the water. And after we had changed, and had walked through the bright lights of the changing rooms, we stood by the edge of the pool. I looked up and saw my mum's face change. Like right there. Her skin was glowing, and her hair, which was tied up in plaits and bundled into a swimming cap, was glowing...

Beat.

She got into the water and came to the side, her arms stretched out towards me. And all her fingers glistening, she called me to jump in. And it was like the water was talking...

Through her...

LEA. Let's go back Nene. Your mum will be waiting /

NENE. I've got to be the one Lea. I've got to be the only one to do that with her.

LEA. You will be. Promise /

NENE. No. Lea we have to go to the pool. I want to show you I want to show her I can do it. Then…

I can do it Lea. I can teach her. Like my mum taught me.
I can change right before her eyes too.

We have to go!

LEA. Erm…

LUNE. I'm in!

LEA. We don't have any stuff.

LUNE. Let's go into the shopping centre. We'll find something there.

Your mum sounds amazing.

You're lucky Nene.

NENE. Lea!

LEA. Nene are you sure?

NENE. Which way?

All exeunt.

8.

DEE *stands on the threshold.*

DEE. It's fine. It was just a trickle…

> DEE *takes a deep breath in.*

> *Beat.*

> The doctor. The new one. Or should I say the last one I saw because I see a different one every time. But this last one…

> He eventually said I should try fresh air after…

> Because I don't know that. Anyway, if it's not the social workers, it is the doctors. Asking to see me. Asking to see her. Asking to just check up on how we are doing.

> *– What did you want to see me about?*

> Well I didn't to be honest. But they told me I couldn't get my repeat prescription until I saw *my* doctor.

> *– Yes. It does appear that Dr Henrys has requested a face-to-face at your next appointment and has left some notes on the system…*

> What *notes*?

> He says nothing.

> So anyone can juss come in here and start reading my notes and talking like they know what I need or don't need.

> *– It is my business after all isn't it.*

> What does he say?

> *– Please don't be alarmed. I want to assure that your notes are treated with the strictest confidence / always.*

> So it wasn't my own GP that actually wanted to see me?

> *– Yes…*

> *– Well…*

> Are you going to write my prescription or not?

– I just wanted to have a chat. Ask a few questions.

I like doctors. I respect them even. But do you know how many questions I have been asked in the last four years.

– Did you not notice anything had changed in her behaviour?
– Not notice her getting…
– And are you sure you don't know who the father is?
– Do you think she knows what's happening to her?
– How is she getting on with the antidepressants?

They ask so many questions sometimes I wonder if they juss go to medical school to learn how to ask questions in a way that makes them sound intelligent.

Eventually he says –

– There is some really interesting research going on at the moment about your condition.

What? Who asked you for research?

– Some of that research suggests there may be a relation between the processing of emotions / and consequently these episodes…

Wow.

– Impressive isn't it?

Can you give me my prescription or not? Please.

– Please. Sit down.

Beat.

– If you were to talk to someone. Find the root of your anxiety. It may well be the end of the nosebleeds…

Talk to someone? Find the root? You are all mad.

– I would like you to consider that we may be able to tackle this another way.

You want to tackle *this*? First by deceiving me to come to an appointment to talk this rubbish at me…

What do you know about what there is to tackle?

A few notes won't tell you anything about me. They won't tell you anything about why I am sitting here and what it is *we* survive every single day.

Did the *notes* tell you about that feeling? Did they tell you that because fear had entered har mouth she did not tell me about the pregnancy until it was too late for an abortion?

Did you read the small print that says that if you are a woman with a pregnant teenager then your whole community will shun you? *That what she was* has now gone. That you can't remember the last time you saw her dance or spend an hour applying make-up like other girls har own age.

I hope you read the bit of the *notes* that tells you that just when you thought it couldn't get any worse, then you start hearing voices. Over and over. And they tell you to find the softest cotton wool and to wrap your daughter up in that thing. You make sure she doesn't have to even breathe on her own. To keep har away from the world because you can no longer trust the world with har life. So you listen to that voice...

And it is like that every day.

Both of you trying to stay above the water of your own island.

And I wish all I had were *notes*. Words that don't really mean anything.

In fact some days I wish all I had was this trickle day in day out. You think this is the worst thing happening to me right now? Blood?

Please give me my prescription. I have to pick up my granddaughter.

There's nothing to *tackle* doctor. It is just a trickle.

I am fine.

DEE *kisses her teeth*.

9.

NENE *and* LUNE *stumble out of a door – fitting with laughter.*
LEA *moaning loudly offstage in the same direction, throws a plastic changing-room tag at them*

NENE *tries to stifle her laughter.*

NENE. Honestly Lea it doesn't look that bad!

LUNE. It fucking does! That's not high-leg, that's a death-by-camel-toe!

LEA *appears from the changing room, now fully dressed again.*

LEA. You're so rude. I thought it was alright /

LUNE. As a tankini!

LUNE *holds out a blue swimming costume to* NENE.

NENE. I'm not going to show you though.

NENE *takes the costume. She goes into the small changing room.* LEA *and* LUNE *wait outside.*

NENE *holds the swimming costume in front of her as she stands looking into the mirror in front of her. The music from the shop changes – 'Dangerous Love' by Fuse ODG featuring Sean Paul plays.*

The atmosphere in the changing room is changing. The lights once bright seem to dim down sporadically. NENE *does not move.*

But she can see 'his' face somehow. See his hands creeping across her shoulders. She can feel 'his' breath on her neck. She can't move. She stays standing there – swimming costume in her outstretched hands. She yelps with fear.

LEA *and* LUNE *jump to their feet.*

LEA. You alright / Nene?

The panic NENE *has been trying to contain is washing over her in waves now – she drops the costume. Holds on to the sides of the changing room.*

Nene?

Beat.

LEA*'s voice is a gurgle of words. All* NENE *can hear is the loud sound of the changing room being ripped from its foundation and washing away. Hands appear around her body and throat. She squirms to get away but is still frozen on the spot.*

NENE. Please!

I don't want this…

It is *my* body…
No.

LUNE. Nene.

NENE. Too close…
And your hands feel so cold…

Beat.

LUNE. Nene!

LEA. Please!

The door of the changing room shakes with LUNE*'s efforts to break it.*

The lock of the door falls apart. The door opens. LEA *and* LUNE *rush in.*

NENE *falls to the ground.*

LEA *rushes towards* NENE *and holds her tight.*

Oh Nene!

LUNE. How could someone have done that to you…

I'm so sorry Nene.

How…

I am lost / for words.

LUNE *slides down onto the floor.*

They did that?

LEA. The song…

I forgot…

NENE. I didn't die.

10.

DEE *stands on the threshold. Arms folded.*

DEE. I remember one day, she is asking if she can paint *me*.
I said –

– *What?*

You want me to sit here as you look at me and paint me?

DEE *strikes a pose as though sitting for a painting.*

I mean I didn't even know she was doing this thing. I never saw har do one painting. But it makes me happy you know. That she has found something. She is doing something with all this *time*.

Her hands trace slowly over the canvas.

I sit down.

And she looks at me. It is almost like this is the first time she is seeing me.

She tells me to lift my head.

– *Lift your head Mum.*

I lift my head.

Wow! This is the first time in years that I have looked up.
I almost cannot hold my head up.
It feels heavy but it feels / so good.

– *Don't look at me.*
Look in the corner if you like.

The corner? That corner filled with all the things I picked up when I worked at the hotel. Anything left behind by guests. Magazines. Business brochures. Reading glasses. All brought back. Here. That corner.

– You can look out of the window / maybe.

Where? There's things / everywhere. Distracting.

– I can't do it if you're looking at me.

I move my head away.

That bit is not so hard. It is a relief in fact.

In the mornings, I hide in my room until har and Babygirl are ready. I never want to get in the way of that. I get dressed and I wait by the door until they have said their goodbyes. And all the time, I look at the ground. I don't want to watch them doing the most precious thing that they can do. I don't have to witness it. The mornings should be juss for them.

So I look away.
From har face.

I can't bear to look at har. I am looking out towards the window. Towards the street. Out of this room…

But I can feel har glowing. And even the greyness of that particular day can't touch her spark.

I am looking at har and I am seeing so much.
So many things that I have words for, and other things that I can't say.

And she, har eyes stuck to that canvas, looks at me back and forth.
And I look at har and she is smiling for the first time in so long.
And I'm hoping that smile on har face is real.
That she means it.
That this is making har happy.
Make har be somewhere else for a while.
See harself in another way.

– Mum you can smile if you like.

Smile?

I don't know how to smile any more Nene.

It will ruin your picture!

– It is your picture. Your portrait. For you.

Smile.

Yes. Like that.

You look…

Tired.
Angry.
Sorry.
A failure / I know.

But in this moment I am feeling so proud.

And P was the one that brought these canvases for her one day. Left them in a bag by the fridge. Said that someone had left them in one of the houses he rents out. He thought maybe Nene would like them. I didn't want to tell him that she was never going to be interested in them. She was thirteen years old, and the only thing she was interested in was hanging out in the park with Lea and buying hoop earrings. I took them because you cannot really say no to P and I hid them in the cupboard under the stairs.

That was the last I saw them. And almost the last time I saw him too.
I think he must have got a new girlfriend and couldn't spend so much time in another woman's house.

Maybe it is a good thing…

Beat.

I asked her where she got the paint and pencils from. They looked like real art pencils you know.

– Lea bought them.

Of course! Those two…

– I hide them. The other drawings. I hide them under the stairs cos I know you never go in there in case of spiders.

It's true. I never go in there now because of the spiders that have taken a long-term lease in my cupboard.

Smile for har I'm thinking.
That might be all I have left to give…
For har.
Har.
She.
Mine.
Har.
We.
Har.

Long beat.

She never has to go out.
She never has to see the world again I tell her.
She can build a new world.
Here.
Inside these walls…
Inside me.
She believes me.
She listens.

Until one day it is too big for her.

For me…

Too much.

DEE *looks at her watch.*

Where is she?

11.

NENE, LEA *and* LUNE *enter as though being pushed/chased by something/someone.*

LEA. You need to check your attitude you hear!
  Your whole face issa disrespect!

LUNE. Lea?

LEA. Did you hear what she said to me though? And calling the security over like…

NENE. But we didn't do anything /

LUNE. Accusing us of being loud? Aggressive?

  I'm fucking sick of this shit.

  LEA *turns to* NENE *who now stands there, blood streaming over her clothes.*

LEA. Oh my god!

  LEA *searches* NENE'*s handbags for the tissues.*

  She starts to mop up the blood streaming from NENE'*s nose.*

  NENE *remains motionless.*

  Nene! I'm so sorry /

  They've done this.

  I can't…

  I should never have brought you out into this fucked-up world!

  Nene? Please you're scaring me.

NENE. It hurts…

LEA. Where Nene?

NENE. Why wouldn't they listen to what you were saying?

  Just believe that I was…

LUNE. It doesn't happen like that.

NENE. The way they spoke to us…

LEA. Always.

NENE. The way they looked at us…

LUNE. Standard…

NENE. They didn't even ask us what happened…

LUNE. Why would they / though?

NENE. You were looking out for me. I told them that.

Beat.

LUNE. Look those bastards are going to get what's coming to them / one day. Karma is the biggest bish I know.

LEA. Are they though?

LUNE. My ancestors have my back / I know it.

NENE. Even if they look at the CCTV and it shows them…

LEA. It doesn't work like that / for us.

LUNE. They do this shit day in day out. I spotted them watching us from time. Checking what we're wearing. What we're holding. Like we're circus freaks…

NENE. You saw that?

I'm sorry /

LUNE. Why though?

NENE. If I hadn't / done that.

LUNE. You think this had anything to do with anything we did?

LEA. They will follow you.

It's that simple.

They don't care that we work and earn our money same way to pay for things the same way they do.

LUNE. They don't care that I've never stolen a damn thing in my entire / life.

LEA. They don't care that you're more terrified of them than they are of you.

LUNE. They don't even care if you're man or woman. Elder or not.

LEA. They don't see us.

LUNE. They see what they want to see / out here.

NENE. Day in. Day out?

LEA. Yes...

And we feel it every day / in here.

LEA gestures a gun to her temple.

LUNE. I won't let them see it hurts though.

NENE. How? How do you hide your pain Lune?

Beat.

LUNE rubs her thigh.

LUNE. You've just got to keep living your best life / and be free. Do bits!

LEA. That's not possible / most times.

NENE. People watching everything you do all the time?

Just because you're *you*?

This outside... this world that I kept dreaming of feeling a part of... this world this is what it does to you?

LEA. Some things are still beautiful...

LUNE. Are they?

NENE. What do they mean *your type*?

– *Troublemakers?*

You were just trying to help me.

LUNE. They will never see that babes.

NENE. I'm sorry…

Beat.

LEA. I think it's about to rain hard. We should / go.

NENE. They should be…

We should be…

LUNE. Seen…

NENE. Like we deserve to be…

Not harassed…

LUNE. Ignored, and neglected…

No different from at home.

The storm gets closer.

LEA. Your mum is cool with you being *you*. I mean you live at home still so she must be /

LUNE. I am loved but she accepts *me* up to a point.

The sky cracks open, and rain falls heavy on them. They don't move.

I want to be seen.

Like I am.

I want my mother to look at me and ask about my friends without being scared I'll talk about *it*.

Or even tease me about who I have a crush on like she does with my sister. Not ask me every day if I really want to have *this* to deal with.

Or on my sister's wedding day, I want to get dressed up and eat and dance and have a room full of eyes watching without wondering why I didn't turn out like my sisters.

I want to still have sleepovers with my cousins. Not be put in another room on my own like some freak.

I want to hear my mother say –

– Lune I hope you find happiness.

Once. Just once. That once will do. But she worries what my life will be...

If she could she...
If she could let me...
I just want to dream, just a little bit...
Of what love I might have in *my* future.
Just as I am...

NENE. You can...

LUNE. I can't...

I will do as they say –

– Hide Lune.
– Shrink Lune.
– Make yourself small Lune.

LUNE *lifts her skirt a little to reveal fresh and healed lines across her inner thigh.*

This flesh...

NENE *moves to hold her hand.*

LEA. This body wants to take up the same space.
I am a good citizen, and I work just as hard.
I deserve a place at your flippin' table.

And when I get up every morning and got to work. Every day 8:59 a.m. I arrive, to a place where, they only talk to me when they want something. Don't think I've got anything to say. Don't ask me what I did last night because of course I was sitting around eating chicken and chatting *street* or *twerking.* Cos that's what we do right? But they don't ask because they don't want to know. Don't dare imagine that there are millions of us out there calling ourselves British reading the same books they read, writing better books, changing history.

LUNE. They ignore that...

LEA. Blank it out and just maybe they'll...

LUNE. Erase us and move on.

LEA. Every day they look at me straight. Straight through me, and ask for another cup of coffee.

   – *If you could be an angel and do that Lea.*

   I can see some days they want to pat me on the head, and tell me '*I'm one of the good ones*' because I'm working. Like I'm something special? Because it's still rare to see a Black face in your shiny boujee offices?

   And little do they know that *we all* have ambition but some of us don't get to fulfil ours because someone is scared by our '*exotic sounding*' name before they read anything else. And another doesn't like the *how loud* we talk during the interview.

   Keep your head down my mum says. Just keep turning up. So she lays out my breakfast every morning. Tea, toast, juice and a serviette. Everything laid out like she's waiting on the Queen. Like I'm doing something important…

   And I want to believe that too /

NENE. Lea you have to tell your mum. You need to leave that place.

LEA. I can't do that to her. I can't let her down again. This is what she dreamt of when she was growing up. That her daughter would one day be out here doing more than she's had the chance to do. More than the cleaning jobs and all the shit she has had to do. She is proud /

NENE. No. She wouldn't want you to feel like this /

LEA. It's not…

   You have your walls Nene /

NENE. They're not *my* walls!

   And there's still walls out here too / Lea.

LEA. *You* can hide Nene but us…

NENE. I'm not hiding / actually!

LUNE. She didn't mean / that…

LEA. Stop telling me what I mean.

Beat.

LUNE. Sorry.

I get it.

Today was meant to be…

LEA. You think I haven't thought about hiding myself away too…

I do.

And I count too.

NENE. You do?

LEA. All the time and I feel like a four most days…

LUNE. Shit!

LEA. Can we go home now?

The shops have almost all shut /

NENE. Why though?

This is my day. Our day. And I'm not ready…

Anyway we need to fill up that thing that Lune has with more of that thing that we were drinking.

LUNE. You mean…?

LEA. Rum?

NENE. I mean that it's my day and I don't want it to stop. Not yet.

And I don't want them to win.

Not yet.

NENE *falls to the ground – she starts to roll across the ground.*

I like it out here.

LEA *and* LUNE *watch her.*

LUNE. Staaaap it!

You're like some gangsta!

Full-fleshed revolutionary...

LUNE *holds out her hand to* LEA.

LEA *grabs it and they dance.*

LEA. Like Naomi Campbell...

And Grace Jones all rolled into one.

LUNE. Like Olive Morris,
And Diane Abbott...

NENE *jumps to her feet, reaches out and grabs* LEA*'s hand.*

NENE. I don't know...

About all these women ...

LUNE. Mary Seacole.

NENE. Her.

LEA. Margaret Busby.

NENE. Her.

LUNE. Malorie Blackman.

NENE. Her.

LEA. Claudia Jones.

LUNE. Baroness Lawrence.

NENE. Her!

NENE *gets increasingly louder during the following speech.*

Her!
Her!
Her!

All three exeunt – NENE*'s voice can still be heard unseen.*

Her!
Her!
Her!

The rain pours hard.

12.

DEE *traces her fingers over the walls in the hallway. The maps.*
The rivers. The streets. The red lines. The blue lines.

Long beat.

DEE. Har!

Just har…

And me…

That's how it's always been.

I want to see har.

Right now.

I want to see har face.

Look at har.

Beat.

She never has to go out.
She never has to see the world again I tell her.
She can build a new world.
Here.
Inside these walls…
Inside me.
She believes me.
She listens.

Until one day it is too big for her.

For me…

Too much.

DEE *looks at her watch.*

Where is she?

ACT TWO

1.

NENE, LEA *and* LUNE *are outside peering into windows of a swimming pool. The dappled light of the water reflecting against their faces.*

They are still soaked to the skin. It is still raining hard.

LUNE *seems to be keeping a lookout.*

NENE. We have to get in.

LEA. Nene we can't. It's closed. Everything is locked up and if we don't go soon, someone is going to see us.

LUNE. Yeah babes. I think we have to leave it. I nearly lost a leg climbing over that fence. I don't think I can take any more.

NENE. I need to…

LEA. We can do it another day.

Look how much you've done today Nene.

NENE. How much you've done for *me*.

LEA. Next time it will be even easier. And we can come to the pool first thing.

Lune you'll come too won't you.

LUNE. This is probably a good time to tell you I can't actually swim. And I haven't worn a swimming costume since school /

NENE. I have to do this!

LEA. Nene. If you get all stressed like in the shop…

LUNE *gets a tissue out of her pocket. Holds it out, waiting.*

NENE. You don't get it Lea.

> He follows me everywhere. The minute I step out of the door just to say goodbye to *my Babygirl*, he's there. Watching. Looking. His eyes… Something *violent* in them. And he smiles.

> Because he knows…

LEA. He's not real /

NENE. He knows I won't do it. I won't tell her…

> Before him, she never really smiled. Not really. She worked hard. She brought me up. Sometimes she swore about my dad and about all men. She held on tight to *us*.

> Then they became friends. He became Uncle P. And sometimes I would get back from school, and I could hear her laughing. Hard. And they would listen to rubbish radio stations and dance. She was happy. And it made me feel good too…

> Sometimes I would dance with them too and he would watch us. Me and Mum dancing. And sometimes, it felt like he was looking in a way…

LEA. You didn't tell me /

NENE. I didn't have the words…

> Then one day, I came home and he was there. And she wasn't. And he said she had given him a key. To *our* house. And that I could keep him company while he was waiting.

LUNE *turns her back to them. Tears stream down her face.*

Beat.

> And I am sick of hiding Lea. That's the only thing he asked me to do before he left. He dropped the keys on the table, and turned to look at me –

– There's no need for anyone to know about this.

Our secret…

I am so sick of hiding.
Of feeling like this…
Always hiding cos something is trying to wash me away.
Pick me up and cast me away.

Sick.
Just sick.
And the pills they give me to help me forget,
Or the ones I take to help me remember to breathe…
They all do the same thing…
They take away *me*.
They subtract and minus the shit out of my *self*.
And I needed it so bad.

And now out *here*?
Today I find out that society is trying to do the same.
So why did I bother hiding?
When everywhere there is someone trying to hold our Black
bodies down. Their rough hands and cruel eyes trying to pin
us down.

Find a way to stay quiet,
– *unseen*
– *smaller*
– *less*
– *muted*

Cos if you don't we'll find a way to kill your spirit, kill your
body, kill your children.

We'll call you names, and twist the truth until –

– *you are the sick,*
– *the angry,*
– *the violent.*
– *Until you build walls…*

– *And as you look through that glass – your only window to
the life we enjoy, we will look right back at you and call
you mad.*

I was never mad Lea.
A *young girl* looking after a child is nothing new until it
happens to you…

But…
Lea…
But now I can see that if I hide myself away, if I fold myself
so small – origami fold after origami fold – I'm doing the
work for them. I'm doing what *he* wanted all along.

So no! Keep your long words to describe what is making me
sick…

NENE *wipes away the tears rolling from her eyes.*

If I become a mermaid again,
We will be safe…
And the maps will be in here…
But out here…
Is where we all belong…
Her…
Me…

Beat.

I'm a Black girl wounded in battle from an early age.
Already mistrusting your every move. Already aware that
my body…

Our young Black bodies should be safe in this world.

LUNE. I am the most beautiful thing my ancestors created and
my lips can kiss fire, and my hands spin gold.

LUNE *looks at her hands. In wonderment.*

I am a piece of beautiful brown magic whose eyes swell at
love, and whose soul never stops dancing…

I am beautiful.

We can be everything!

LUNE *exits.*

LEA. Can we though? All we have to look forward to is a life of
playing small? Dumb? Is that it? Like we've not seen what
they did to our parents and our grandparents? I can't do it
Nene. I can't shrink any more.

I can't keep working harder just to exist. Mum will get that.
She'll hear that won't she?

Just cos they keep taking our goodness and making it
something ugly, doesn't mean we shouldn't keep rising.

I have come with new seasoning. Different words. New
words to fill the silence.

Please don't speak to me like that.
I'm allowed to fail too.
I like shepherd's pie actually.

NENE. Lea how can I make you happy?

LEA. –

> NENE *takes her phone out of her pocket.*

> *'Dangerous Love' by Fuse ODG featuring Sean Paul plays*
> *from it.*

I'm going to dance to it. It was my favourite song. And Mum
loved to watch me dancing...
I want to dance for *her.*
I want to remember how *she* looked at me.

The sound of breaking glass.

We have to draw a new map.
Find new words...

LEA. And I want to have fun Nene. Just sometimes. Just fun.

NENE. My mum used to tell me a story about a mermaid...

> LUNE *enters holding a stick/pole in her hands.*

LUNE. I may have found a window.

NENE. I feel like an eight right now!

> LEA *and* LUNE *exeunt.*

> NENE *dances to the song – arms outstretched, light beaming*
> *from her.*

2.

The front room. DEE *sits on top of one of the mounds of junk in the corner of the room.*

Throughout this speech she slowly climbs down.

DEE. Close your eyes.

Close your eyes and sleep will come.

But she juss looks at me. Eyes wide. And I can't get har to go to sleep so I read the books she likes. The same ones she hears every day but still no sleep. She is stubborn like that, so I start to sing but she says –

– No Granny don't sing!

DEE *kisses teeth.*

So I tell her I'm going to tell her the only story that matters to us. The same one my grandmother would tell me. And she juss keeps looking at me…

And for that second, I don't know if I can tell it again. If I will always remember it the way I first heard it. I wrote it down once so I would never forget the story. I was worried I was getting Alzheimer's after I went shopping one day and forgot my bra in the changing room. That's when I ran home, my breasts swinging like soft pendulums, and wrote it all down. It's somewhere here…

DEE *starts searching for the story throughout the following speech. As she searches, her frustration grows, but we can hardly hear that in the soft way she tells the story.*

But it seems, I can still remember and so I tell her –

There once was a young king. The king was famous across his land on the edge of one of the most beautiful forests in Nigeria for his strength and bravery. He would lift a bull with one hand and fight a hundred men with one single hand. Every man wanted him to marry their daughter.

But the king was too busy fighting to care about girls or such things as romance, and courting and picking flowers. Many women were brought to his house, to dance for the king in the hope that one day he would choose someone to be his wife. But still the king was not interested. Then one day as he crossed the plains of his beloved country back to his home, after another successful battle, he saw in the distance a great warrior.

A fighter. Someone strong and skilful who was practising their sword dance alone. The king was worried that there was another warrior who might one day challenge him, so he hid in one of the many big trees to watch this warrior in action. He saw that the warrior had the smallest face. The warrior's skin shone in the light of the day, and the warrior's lips were shaped as though ready to be...

The king could not believe his eyes when he got close enough to look at the mighty, skilled swordsman and realised that the warrior was in fact a young woman.

– *Girls can have swords too my dear...*

The king went to move closer. To tell her to stop. To go back to the other women but before he knew it...

He could not move. His eyes could not stop looking at her, his heart beat faster than his own mother beat yam...

– *Yam is a vegetable.*

He stood there watching until the sun began to set, and the warrior packed up her things and headed home. The king followed and when she walked through the door of her house, he walked in too. He called to the family, and asked to speak to the father.

Her father was an old man. Close to the road of the ancestors.

– *It's not a real road. It is like a place where old people go.*

The father was pleased when the king insisted that he marry the daughter and make her queen. But there was a problem. The father explained that his daughter had been promised to a spirit who had visited their home no more than a year before.

– Spirit…

Ehem!

Juss listen…

The spirit promised to let her stay with her parents for one year more but would be back to collect his bride.

The young daughter had been in training ever since to fight off the spirit if he returned.

The king laughed at this. Asked the young daughter to pack her things, and assured the father that should the spirit return, he would fight it off and the daughter would have no need to fight for her life any more.

The father pleaded. He said that the spirit had made sure that if she got married to anyone else that any children they bore would never feel the love of her father. And would bear the mark of the promise.

– Babies?

Yes…

They come from…

Ask your mummy.

The king was not listening. He was now deep in love. So away he rode with his new bride-to-be, and after no more than three days back in his land, they got married. She became queen of the beautiful, wondrous land.

Some time later, the queen announced that she was having a child, and before long the baby was born.

A beautiful baby girl. A beautiful baby girl with a small mark on her back. The queen thought nothing of the birthmark but the king saw it as a bad omen.

– Yes she was a baby.

So on the first night after their new baby daughter arrived, the king turned away. The second day the king refused to hold the baby, and on the third day, he ordered the queen to either leave the baby with someone else or go and live with the baby on the other side of the land.

The queen was so sad but she could not abandon her daughter. So they lived away from the king, and the queen brought up her daughter alone with a little help from the other women. But every day that passed she could see that the scales on her daughter's back had started to grow all over her body.

Then after nearly a year small fins appeared on either side of her chest, and in another two years, her daughter was barely able to breathe as her mouth had turned into an almost perfect small pout.

The queen tried hard to not believe what was happening. But one day as the women sat around a fire talking, a wise woman turned to her –

– *Nwanne m nwanyi, your child is cursed and you must do the right thing*.

The queen replied –

– *What is the right thing? She is my child* –

– *Take her to the river. Put her in it. If she swims away like a fish, then let her go. If she just starts to drown then pick her up, but either way you will know.*

The queen was very troubled by this idea. But the following morning, earlier than birds, before the sun could blind the truth, she got up and bundled her baby in the bluest *wrapper* she could find, took her daughter to the edge of the river. She cried. She cried like she had never cried before.

DEE *wipes away her own tears.*

She put her daughter slowly into the water, and before her very eyes, her daughter's legs joined together to make one long tail, and her skin was shining brighter than it had ever shone before. And without a single goodbye, her daughter swam away.

Every day the queen would go back to the same edge of the river. And she would cry her tears into the water that took her child away.

But her daughter was now known as the most beautiful goddess, and it became a thing of luck to catch a glimpse of her tail on the horizon of any river or sea.

And everybody to this day still calls her Mami Wata.

3.

LEA *and* LUNE *stand on the edge of a pool. The dappled light of the water reflecting its shadows across their faces and bodies.*

Long beat.

LEA. I feel…

LUNE. What has happened to me?

LUNE *looks hard at her leg.*

LEA. Something in there…

LUNE. My scars…

LEA. We don't have to talk about it…

LUNE *runs her hand across the scars during the following speech.*

LUNE. This is what I used to feel…

Like every day I am being cut up by words, looks…

And now…

I can see my whole self. And these scars…

All I see are ripples on my skin…

That's what they are Lea. Ripples to remind me that I am still floating. That this body is still moving…

My head is above the water…

And now I'm out…

Maybe *they* need to be out too. Maybe my mum will see them and… I don't know what she'll say Lea… I don't know…

LEA. They're beautiful Lune.

Beat.

LUNE. Lea you're looking…

LEA. Golden?

Yes I know.

Beat.

Where's Nene?

LUNE. She hasn't come up yet.

Beat.

They both peer into the water again.

LEA. Can you see her?

LUNE. No…

Lea what / if…

LEA. Just keep looking!

Long beat.

4.

DEE *stands on the threshold*.

DEE (*whispering*). Come back Nene.
   Otu nwa m…
   Please…

   I'm trying not to worry you know.

   Maybe this is normal…
   Maybe this is what normal feels like.
   I don't know…
   She always puts her daughter to bed.
   She wouldn't miss putting her to bed.
   She misses too many other things.

   I don't know any more if I want *normal*.

A single drop of blood falls from DEE's *nose*.

5.

LEA *and* LUNE *pacing at the edge of the water*.

Long beat.

LEA. What am I going to tell her mum?

LUNE. She has been in there a while now…

   Fuck Lea you don't think…

   Maybe we should call someone? I can go out there and try to
   get help –

LEA. Can you not do any drama right now Lune?

LUNE. It's just when was the last time she went swimming?
   Does she even know how to be in water any more?

LEA. Yes.
   No.

I don't know…

Today was a mistake and I don't know why I couldn't just leave it. She was happy staying at home.

LUNE. *I know this is bad but you can't mean that…*

LEA. You don't know Nene. You can't get it –

LUNE. Someone and something she can't even see takes away who she can be every day.

Yeah you're right I don't get it…

LEA. Please Lune…

She's been under for so long. And I can't bear to go back in to find her…

Beat.

LUNE. She's a mermaid remember?

LEA. No. She's not. She's my really sick friend. She's the girl that has a chair by the window that never moves. She's just this fragile thing who can't breathe in this world right now…

LUNE. What was that?
Did you hear it?

LEA. No.

Beat.

LUNE. There!

In the deep end…

The light reflects differently.

Is that her?

LEA. Oh my god!

LUNE. If she can breathe underwater… she can learn to breathe anywhere.

6.

DEE *is on the threshold of the house – she is pacing.*

DEE. It's her. Nene.
My girl.
My Nene.

– Who is she?

She is *my* daughter. She's gone missing I think.

– How old is she?

Eighteen. Almost nineteen. One week away from nineteen.
Not really an adult…

Beat.

– Does she frequently go missing like this?
– Do you know which friends she's with?
– Is there a particular place they like to hang out?
– Has she been behaving strangely in any way recently?

DEE *laughs out loud – a laugh so close to tears it sounds like crying.*

You don't understand anything.

She should have been home a long time ago.

She should be back by now.

And look at it out here! Look at the rain!

I think something terrible has happened / officer.

No I don't want a cup of tea.

Can you not hear me?

I won't calm down…

Beat.

No I am not okay.
I am not fine.

Something terrible must have happened.

Please.
I couldn't keep her inside...

7.

LEA *and* LUNE *are still standing motionless, looking into the water.*

NENE *appears. Eyes big. Skin glistening. The water reflecting all over her.*

LEA. Oh my gawd Nene what the fuck?

NENE. It was...

LUNE. You look...

LEA. I thought...

NENE. In there...

LUNE. Beautiful.

NENE. I saw them...

   They told me *things*.

LEA. What *things*?

NENE. Well they didn't tell me exactly. They sang it. Songs
   I could understand... I think...

LEA. Who Nene?

NENE. They sang about never travelling alone. They move in
   groups. In shoals or in schools. They have to, to protect
   themselves. They told me to never be alone. Songs about the
   scales they carry on their back. Songs about the salt on those
   scales and of every ocean, every river they have ever swam
   in. And why a whole ocean on our backs does not have to be

a burden. They can be bright and soft and light. That their softness…
Can protect too.
We have to protect our softness…
They sang to me of how they shine so the other mermaids know that they can shine too.

LEA. You're not making sense / Nene.

LUNE. Sssshhh!!

NENE. We need each other. Whole shoals and schools. Side by side. And even when we are swimming against the tide, the *force* of us…
Protects.
Our soft armour doesn't need to change. No matter what the world tells us. There is nothing wrong with being soft Lea. They told me that. There's nothing wrong with *us*…

Women who look like us…

A police siren can be heard at close proximity.

We can be our own shoals. Schools. We can travel side by side and we can survive… we can breathe better even.

Shadows appear.

LUNE. I think we need to go…

LEA. You look and sound like my twinny again.

NENE. Lea you'll always be my twinny but you need to let me look after you sometimes.

I'll always be here…

Shadows get closer.

You can have your stories too y'know.

8.

DEE *sits on the edge of the sofa in her front room.*

A door closes.

NENE *enters.*

NENE. Mum…

> DEE *kisses her teeth.*

DEE. That's all you have to say for yourself is it?

NENE. How is she?

DEE. Fine.

> She's like you; she sleeps like a plank of wood.

> Why are you standing there dripping with water? Where
> have you been Nene?

NENE. I'm sorry / Mum.

DEE. I've called everyone.

> The police.
> The hospitals.
> The fire brigade.
> Mountain rescue /

NENE. What?

DEE. Don't *what* me?

> What was I meant to think? What?

> You want to kill me with worry?

> You go out and you don't come back until this time. And
> then the police bring you back. You go out for one day and
> come back a criminal? Is this what you want from your life
> to be a criminal? Is this how you impress your friends these
> days? Eh eh!

NENE. No. It wasn't like / that.

DEE. I cried.

> I even prayed.

NENE. We were just…

> The alarm only went off when we tried to find towels…

> The police are making a big fucking drama out of nothing.

DEE. So now you're swearing as well? Is this how you and your new *gang* talk?

NENE. It isn't a gang!

DEE. I don't know what I would have done if anything had happened / today.

NENE. I'm here now…

DEE. You had a good day?

> What did you do then apart from getting arrested?

NENE. Not arrested. Not even a caution.

> *Beat.*

> Mum can you look after Babygirl again tomorrow?

DEE. Again?

NENE. I said I would go to the nail shop with Lea and Lune.

> Lea will meet me here though cos…

DEE. What are you talking about?

NENE. I am going out that door tomorrow.

> We're doing bits Mum!

> DEE *can barely hide a smile.*

DEE. *Bits?* What is this *bits*?

NENE. Lune says it all the time. I can't wait to tell you about Lune. She's amazing! Out there everyone is saying it. And now I'm saying it. I like it. *Bits.*

> *Beat.*

DEE. Yes. I can look after har. Once you have done your *bits* here.

I'm going to clear the kitchen. Then in here...

This whole place needs to be done before the social workers come back next week. I'm tired of their questions!

NENE. Let me do it.

I can do the maps too...

DEE. The maps?

NENE. Maybe...

NENE goes to exit. On her back, an iridescent strip of skin/scales flashes through.

DEE. What is that on your back?

NENE. Something from...

The water?

NENE tries to catch sight of her own back.

DEE. Maybe...

NENE. Want to dance with me?

Beat.

DEE. You want to dance?

NENE holds her arms out. DEE grabs hold of them and stands up.

NENE. Mum there's something I want to tell you...

DEE. Yes?

NENE. Not today...

DEE holds her face and kisses her cheeks.

I'm going to find the laptop. There's a song that Lune's mum listens to that I think you'll like...

NENE exits.

Beat.

DEE. Tell me to live without har.

Tell me to imagine a day without har.

Tell me to see beyond that big thing in my chest that started growing the day she was born.

Oceans cannot contain it.

I dare you to tell me to know anything else but har.

Tell me to not dream all my dreams for har!

Her.

Music – 'Offence' by Little Simz plays from behind her.

NENE *enters. They dance.*

NENE *counts throughout their dance.*

NENE. One...

Two...

Three...

Four...

Five...

Six...

Seven...

Eight...

Nine...

The End.

www.nickhernbooks.co.uk

facebook.com/nickhernbooks

twitter.com/nickhernbooks